You can scan and print pictures for personal use so you can color them multiple times or print on a different type of paper.

This book belongs to :

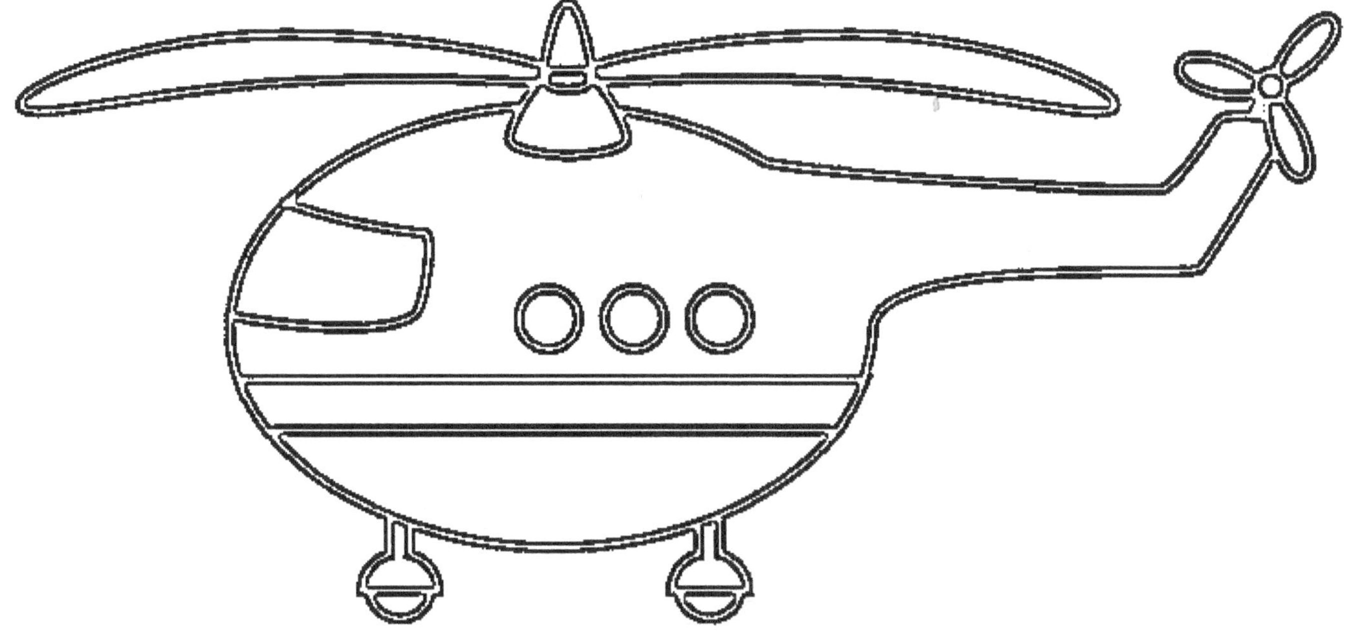

Repaint and colorize it here

Repaint and colorize it here

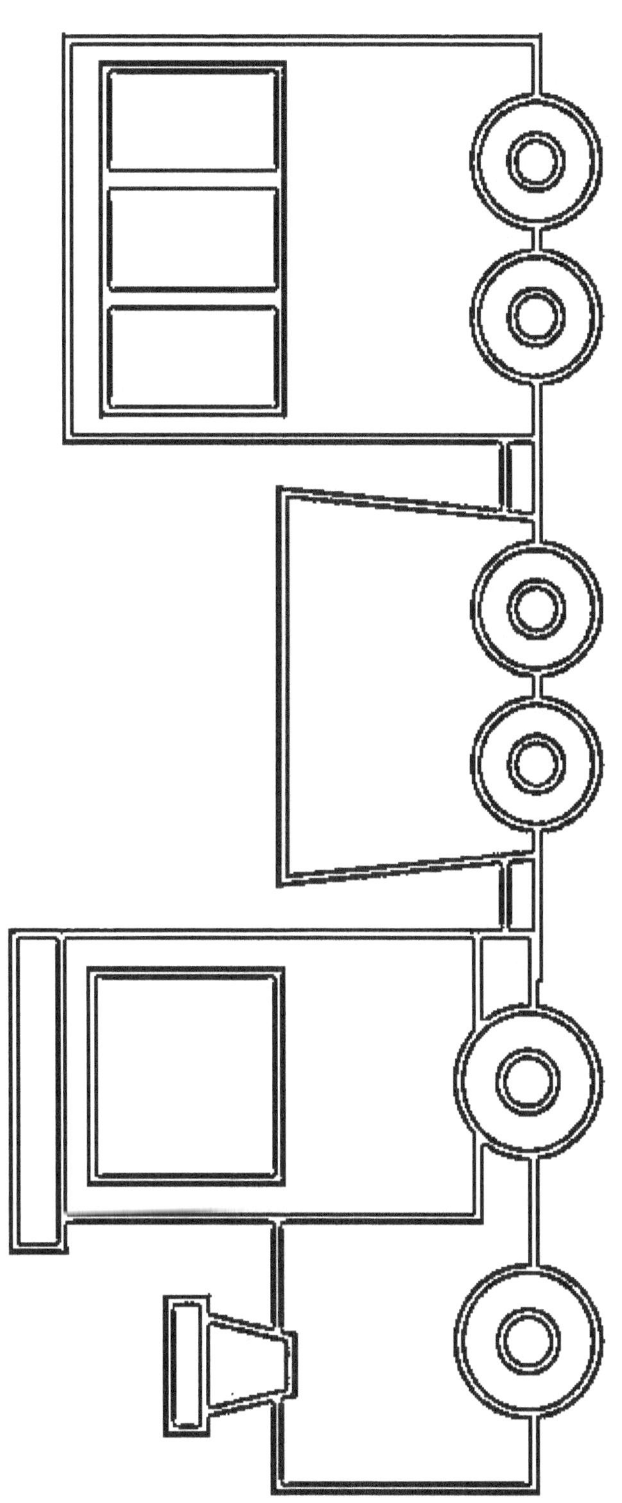

Repaint and colorize it here

Repaint and colorize it here

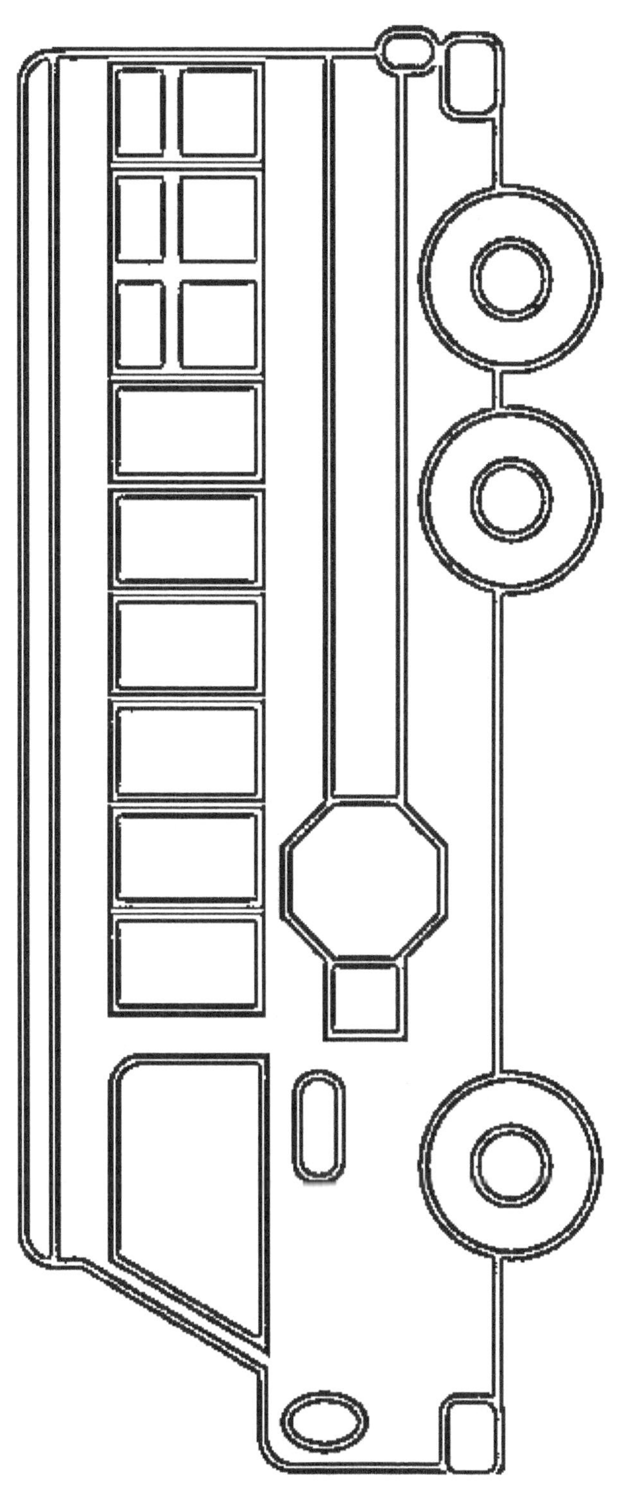

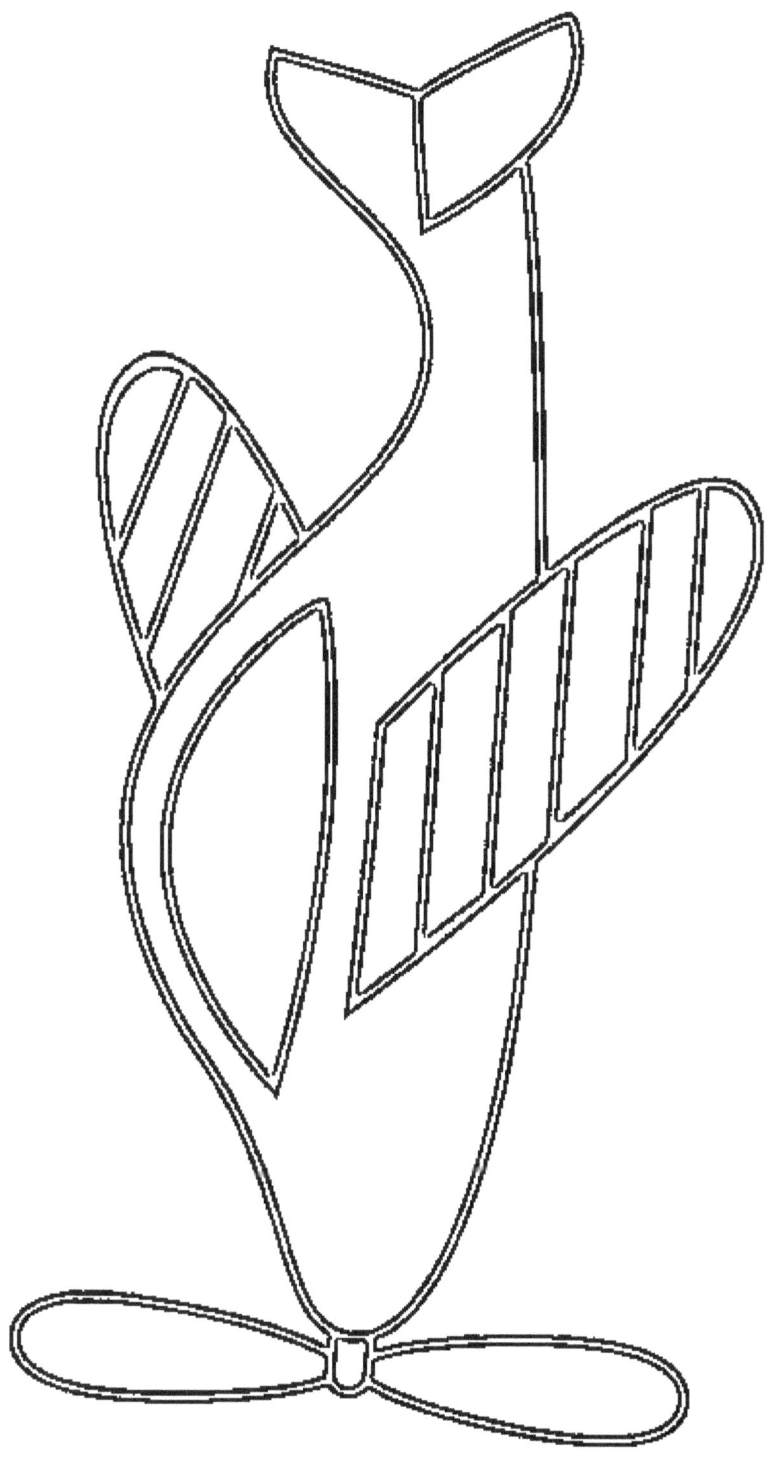

Repaint and colorize it here

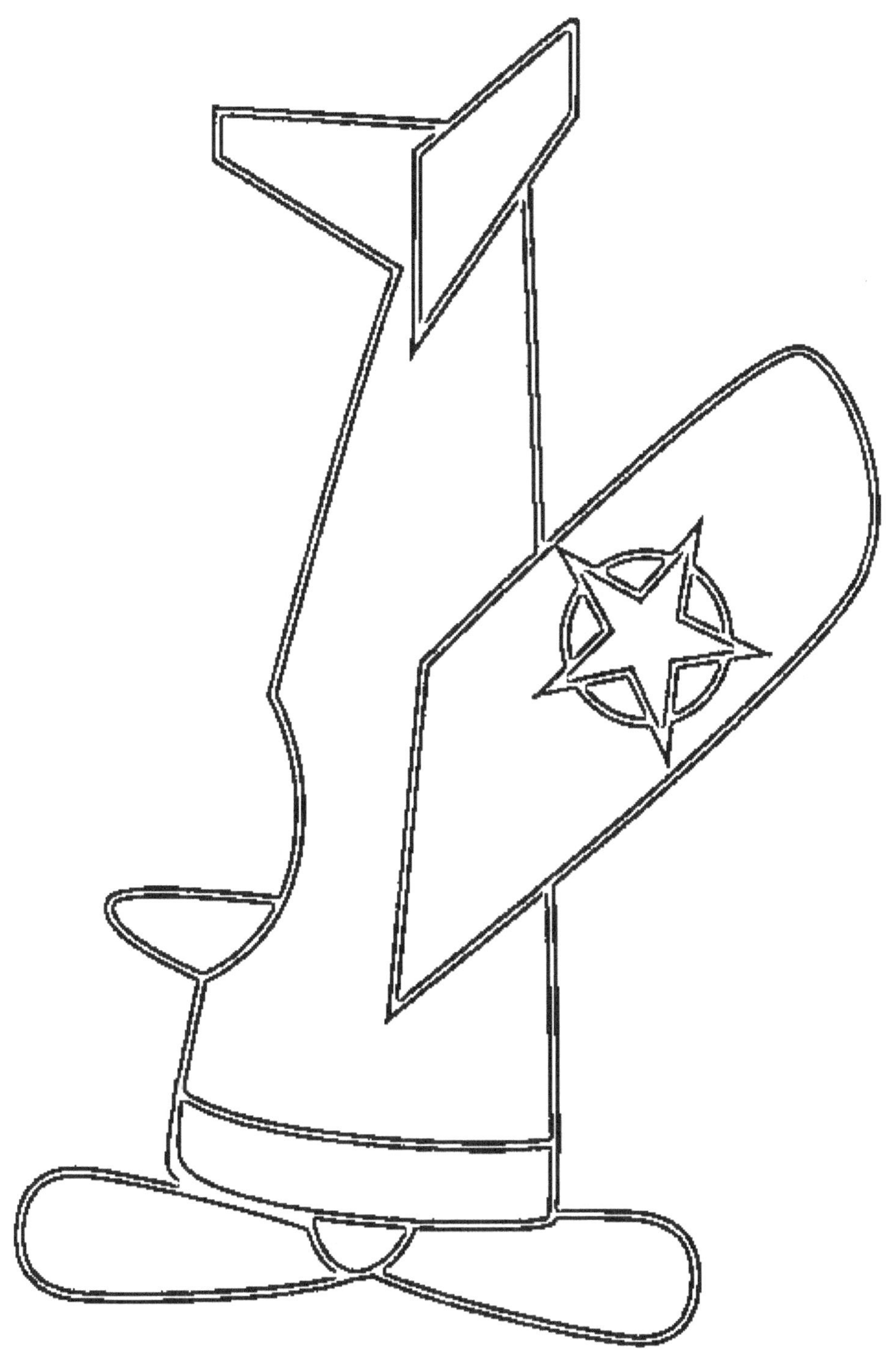

Repaint and colorize it here

Repaint and colorize it here

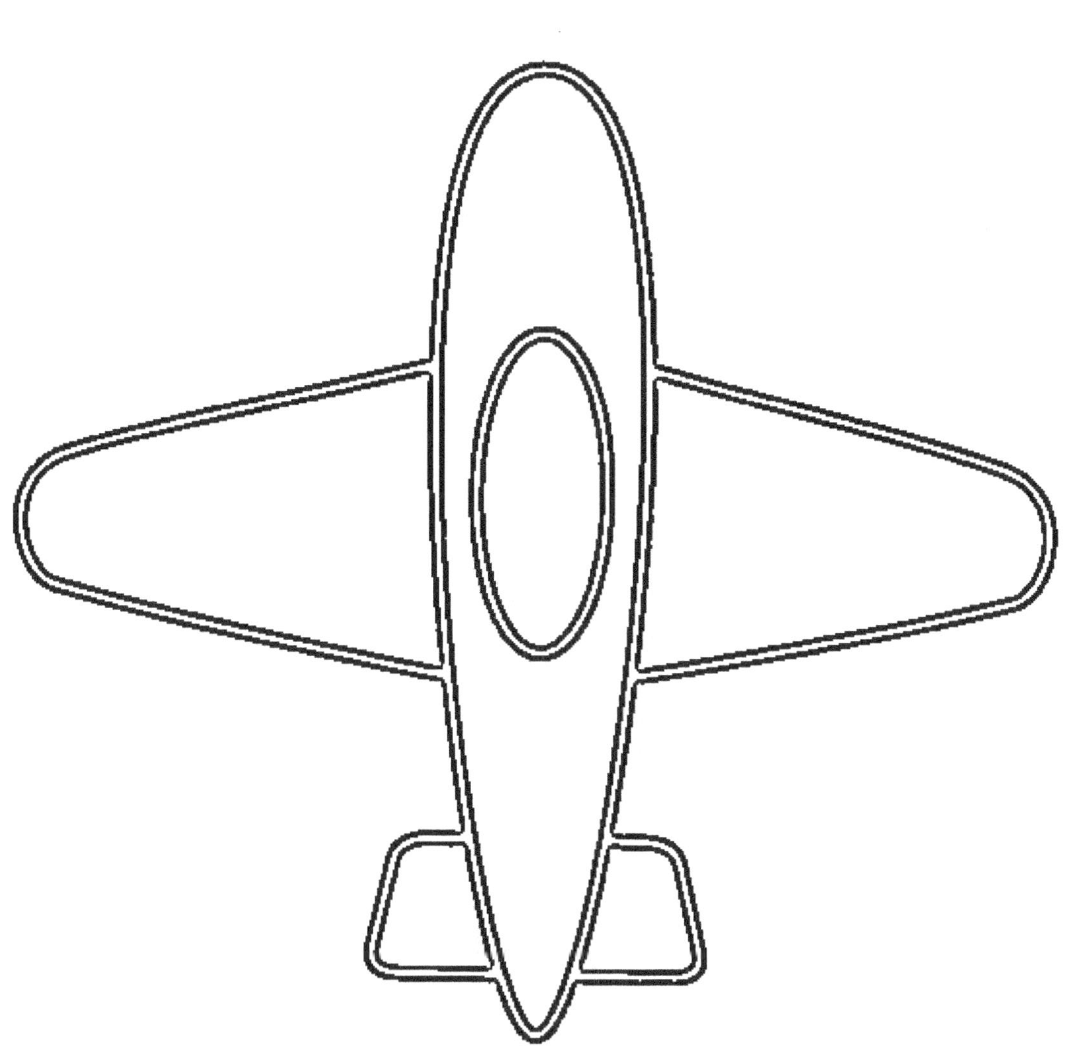

Repaint and colorize it here

Repaint and colorize it here

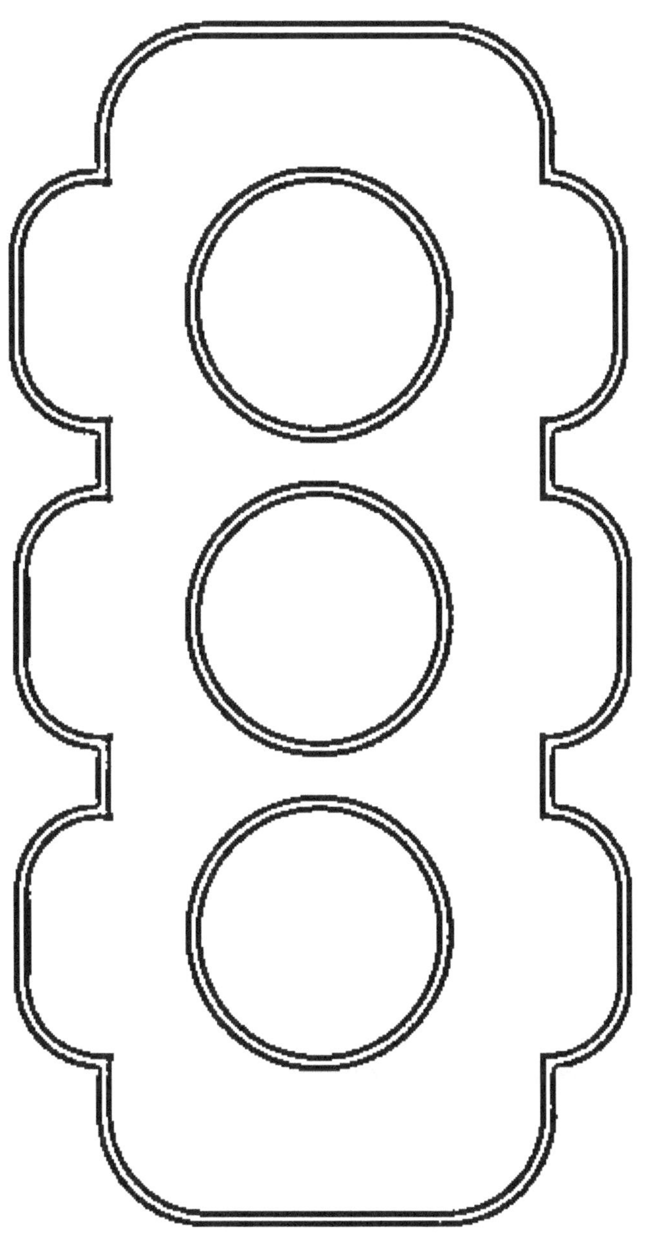

Repaint and colorize it here

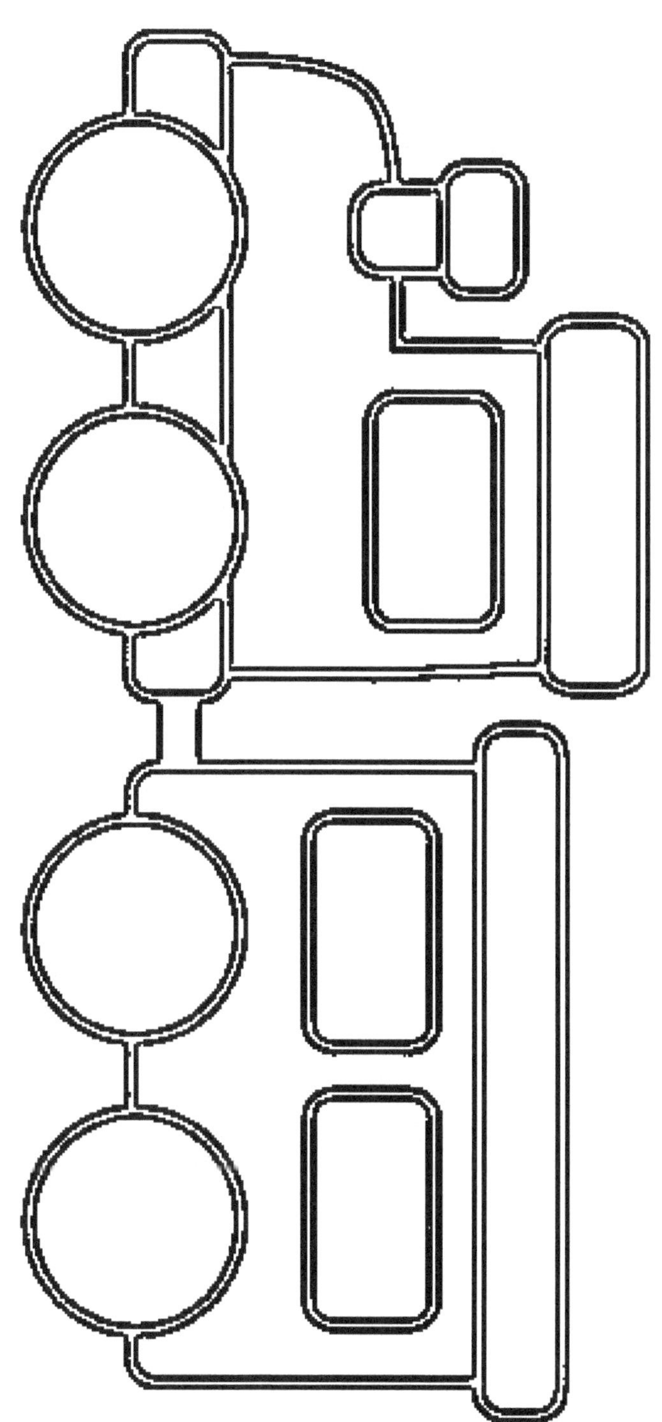

Repaint and colorize it here

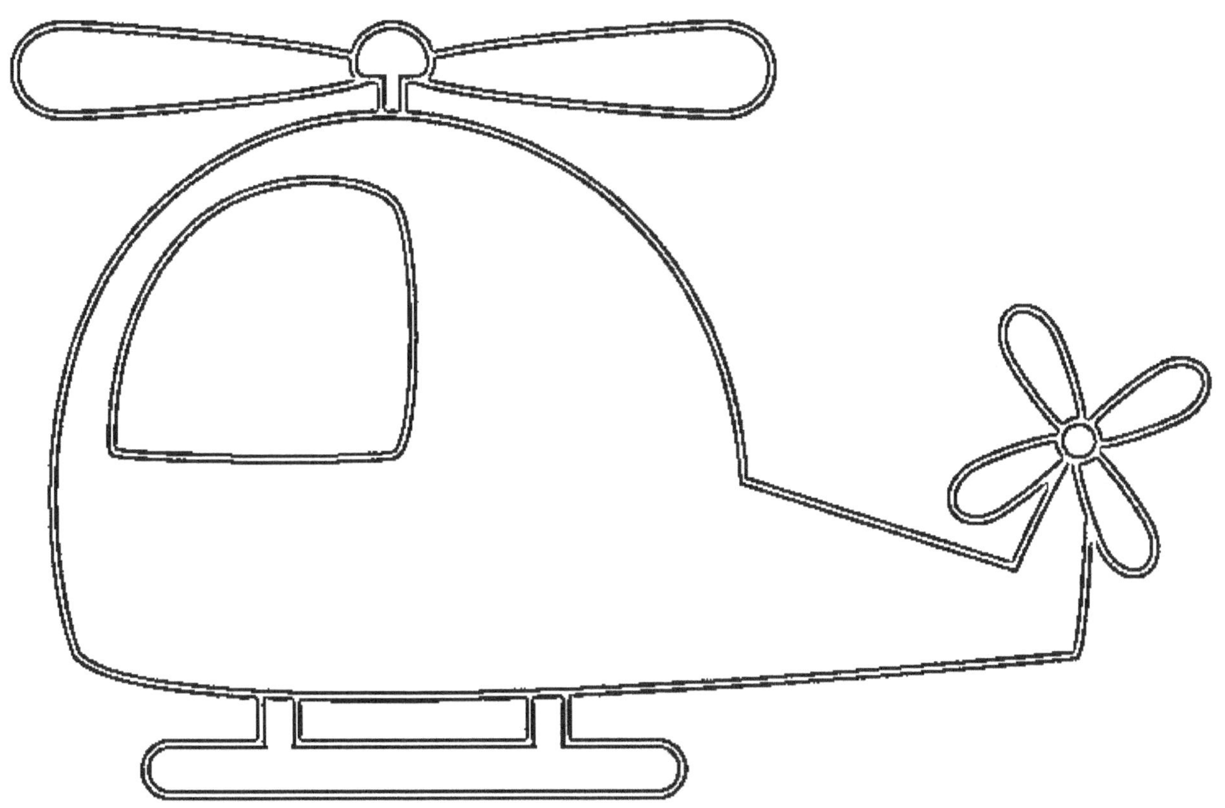

Repaint and colorize it here

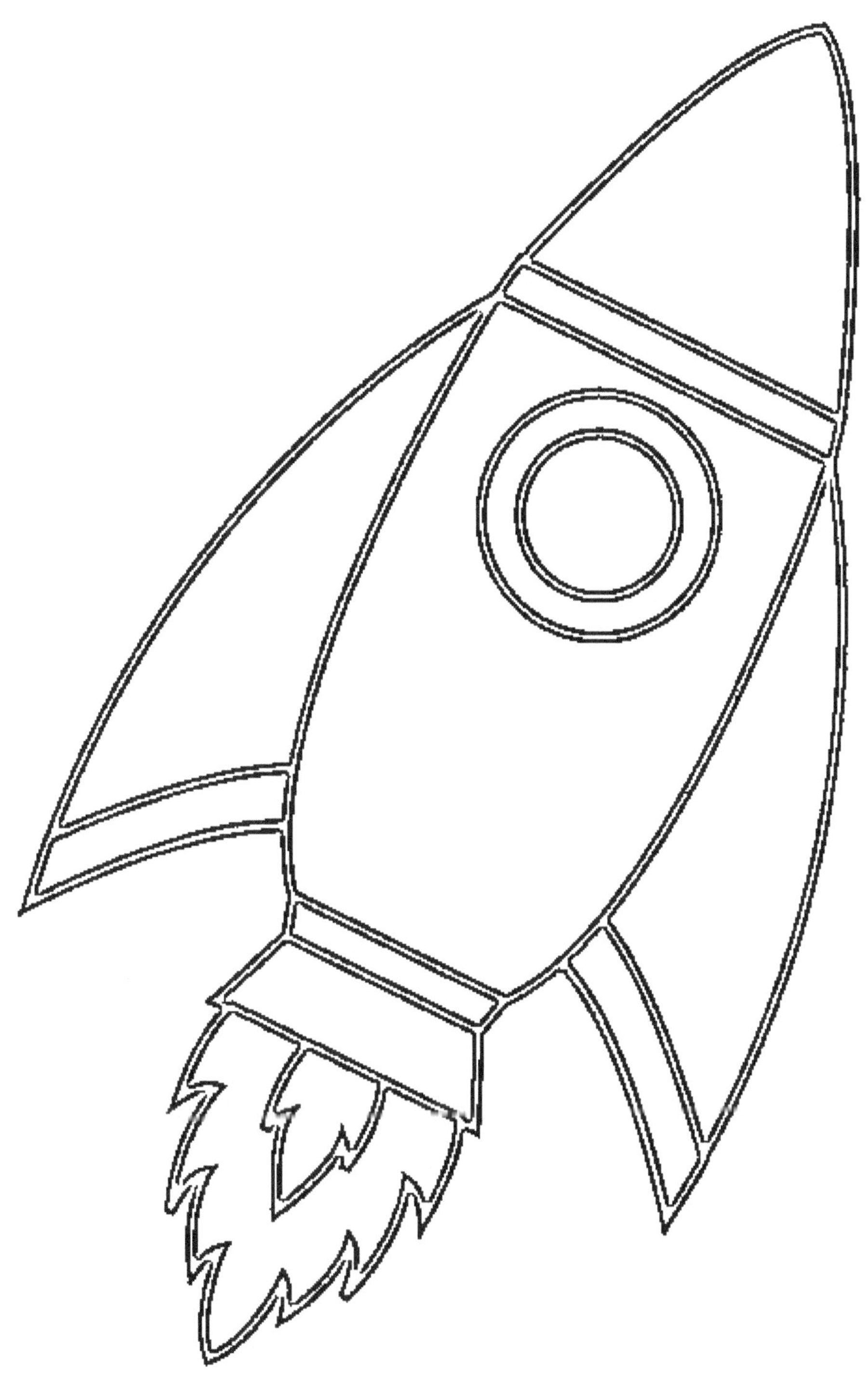

Repaint and colorize it here

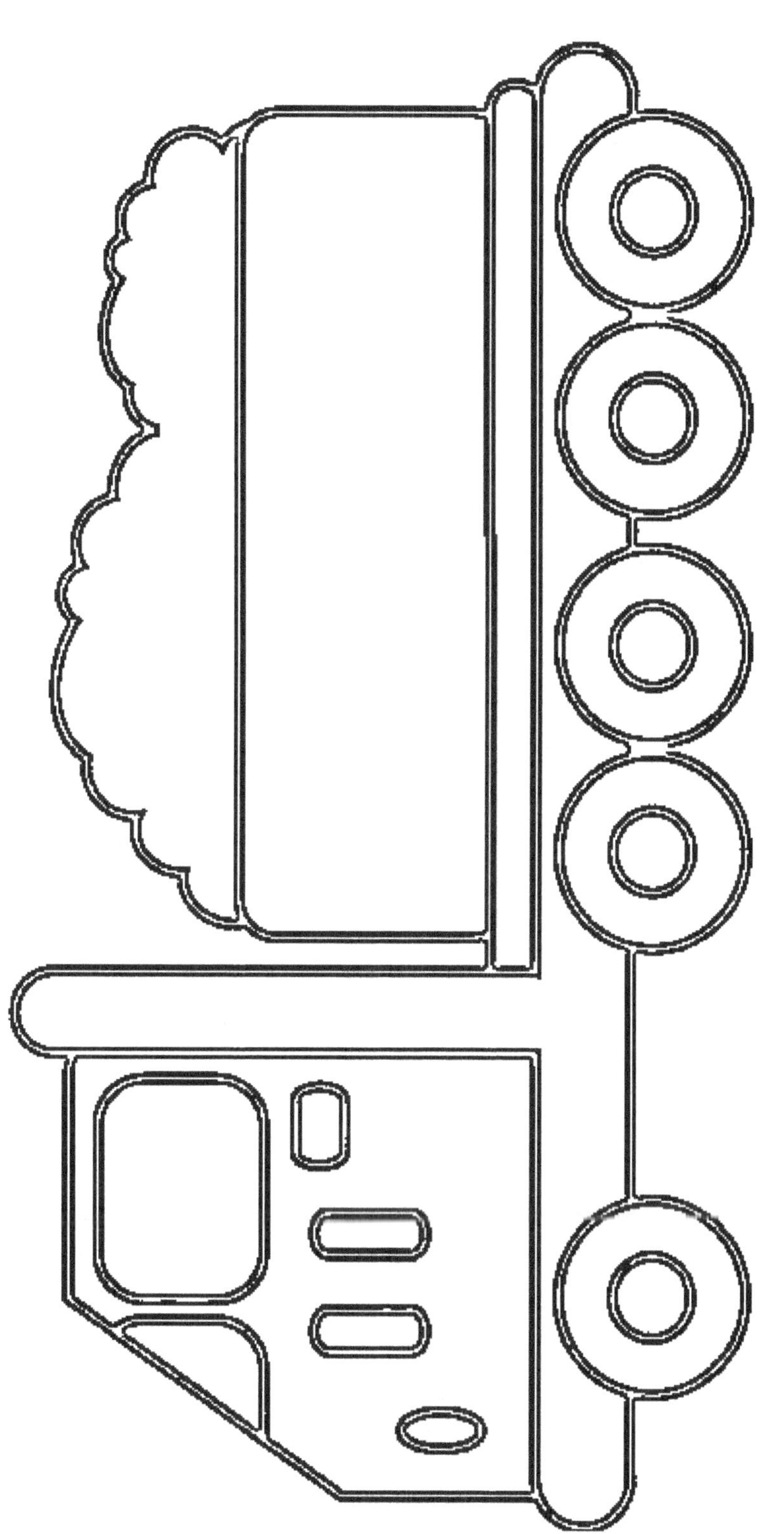

Repaint and colorize it here

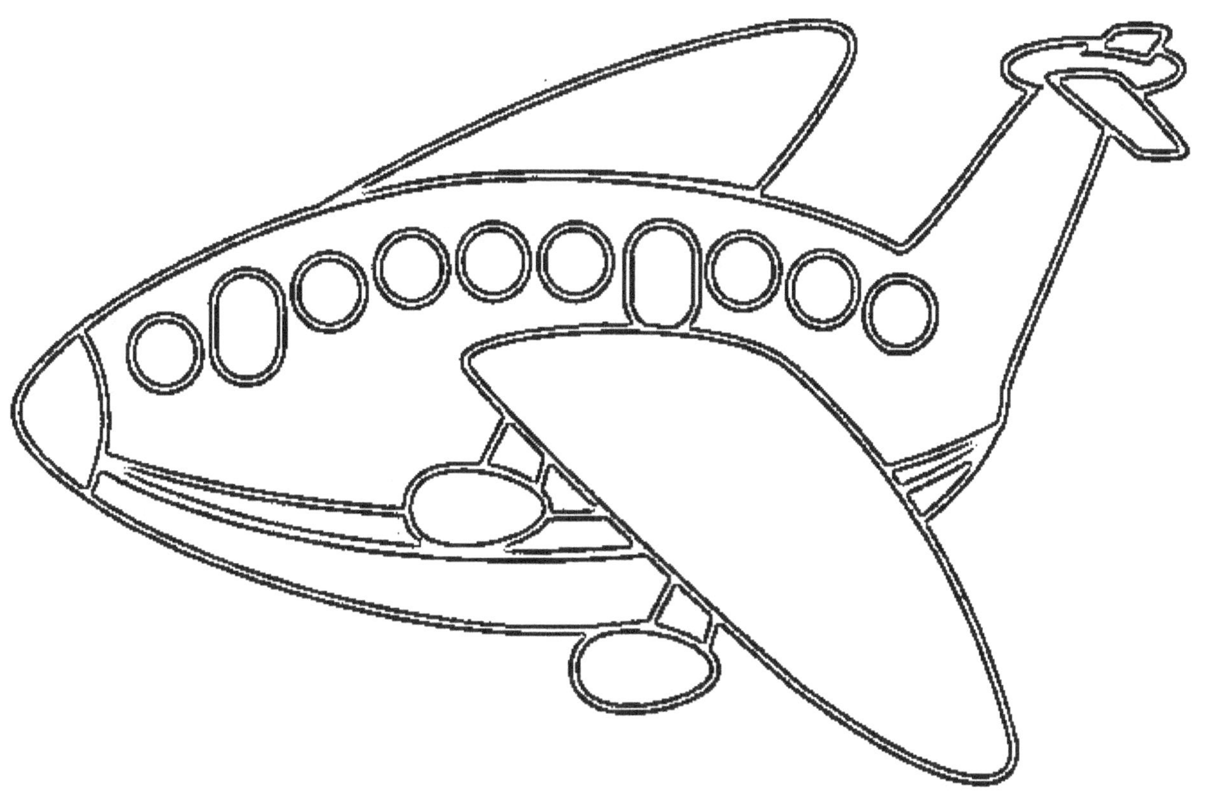

Repaint and colorize it here

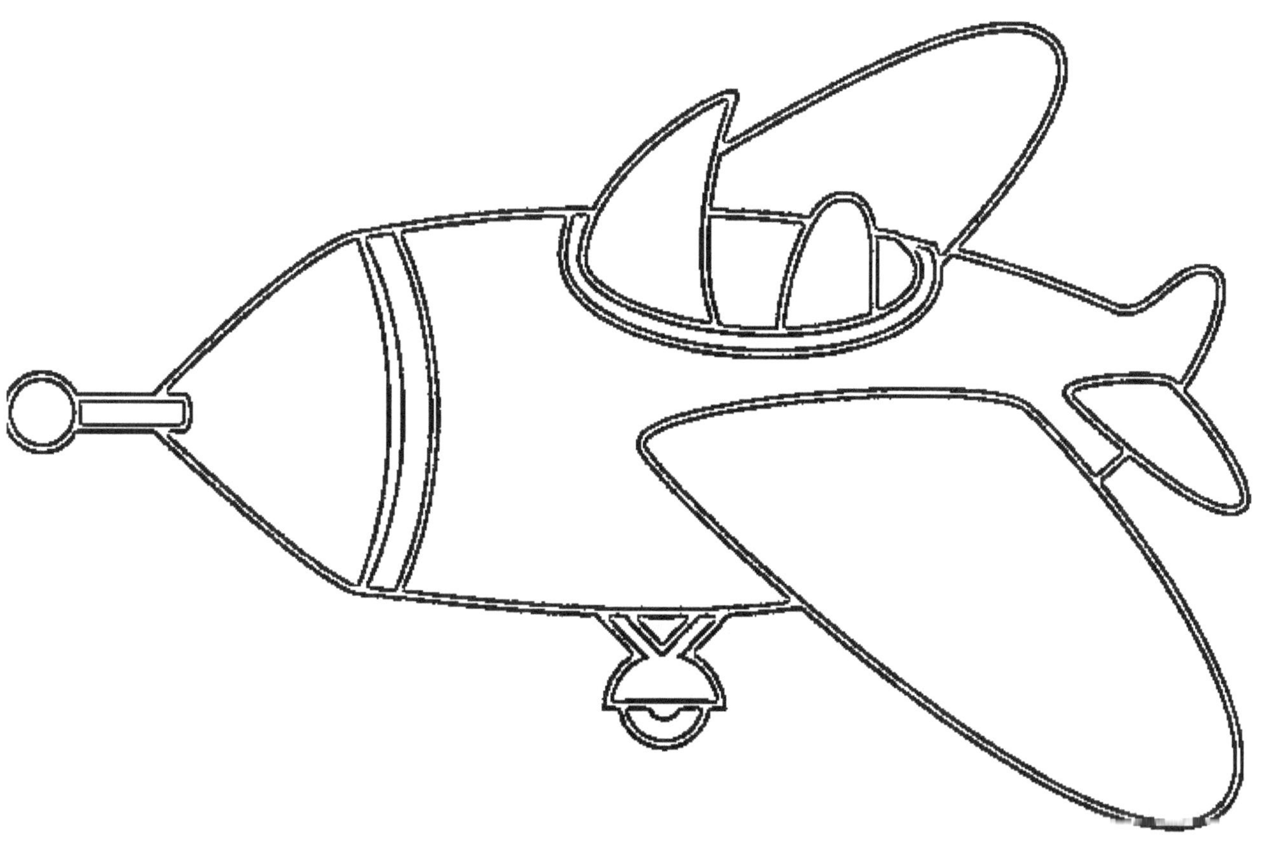

Repaint and colorize it here

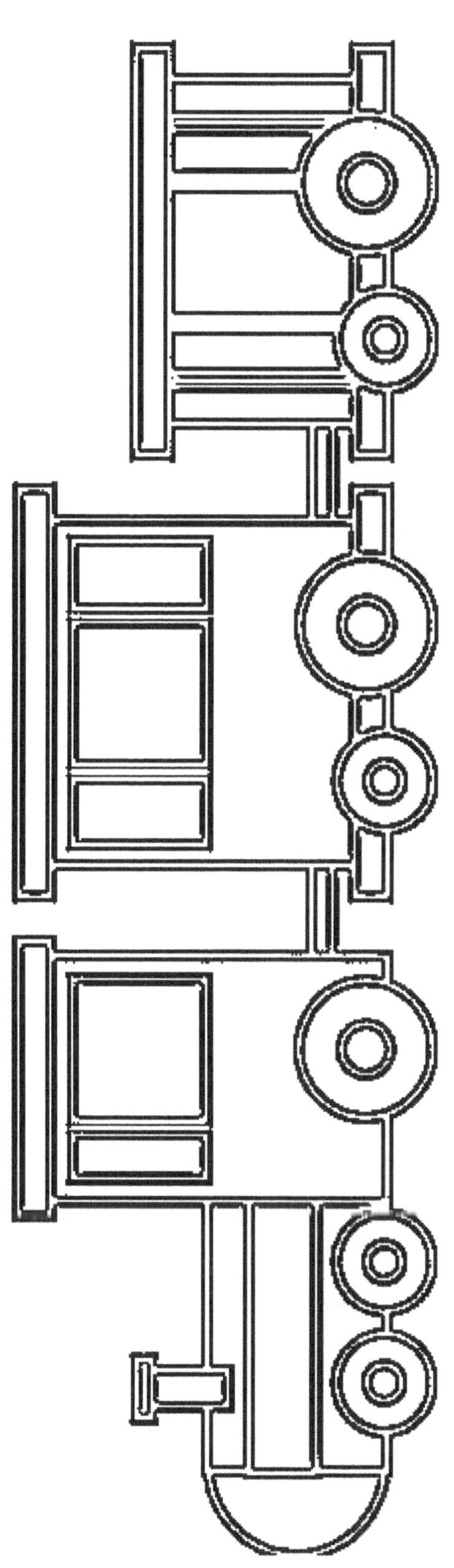

Repaint and colorize it here

Repaint and colorize it here

Repaint and colorize it here

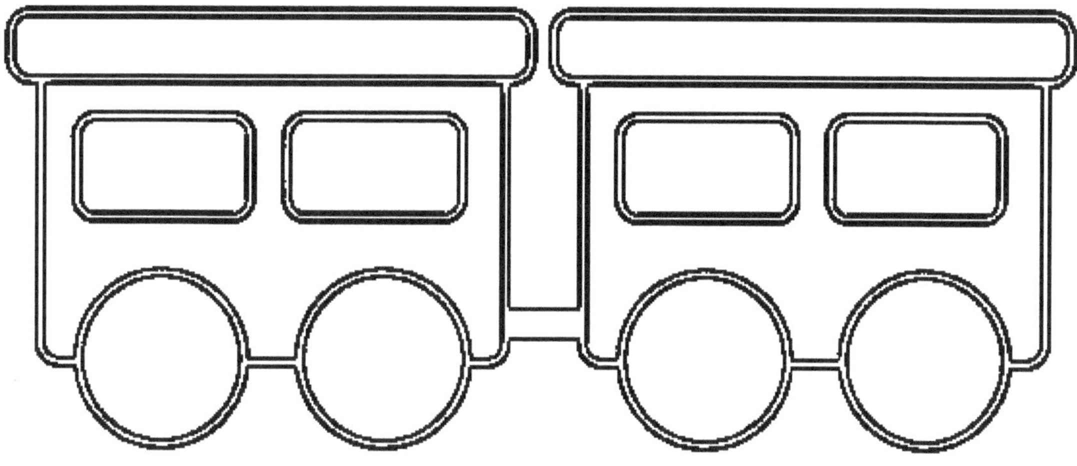

Repaint and colorize it here

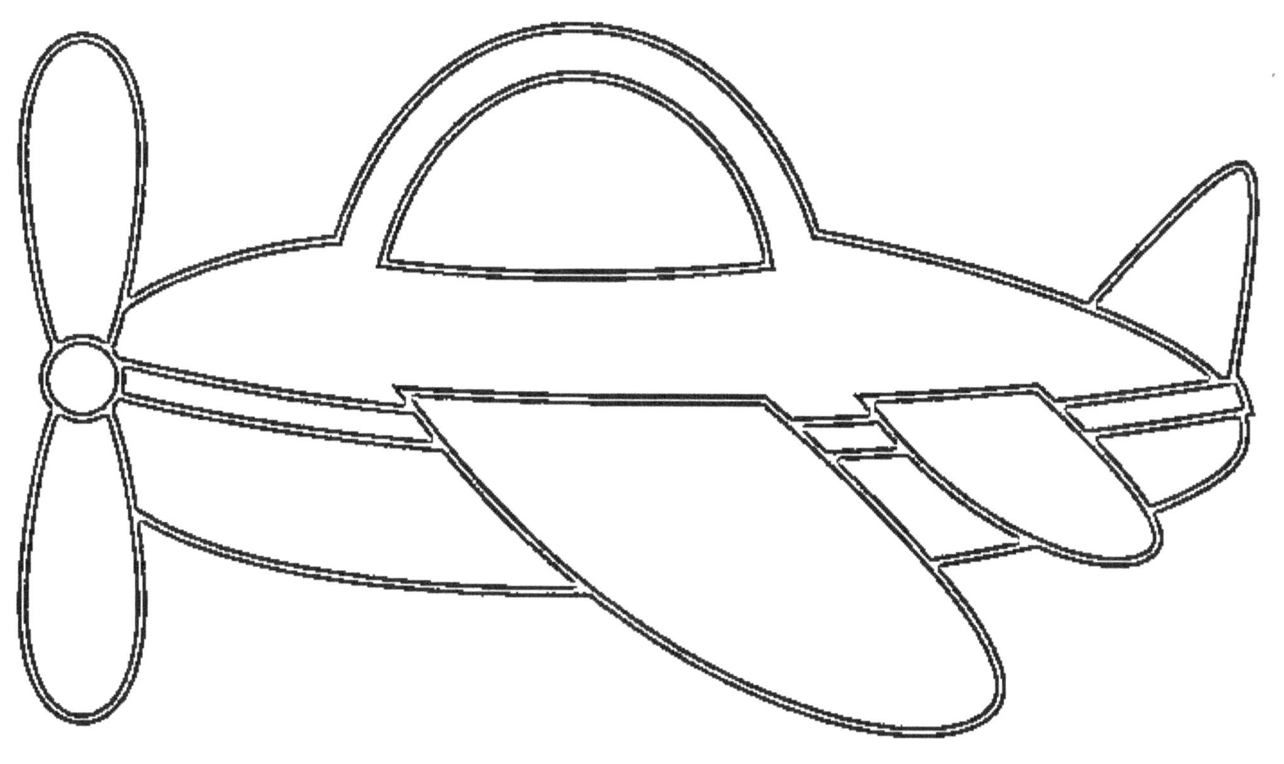

Repaint and colorize it here

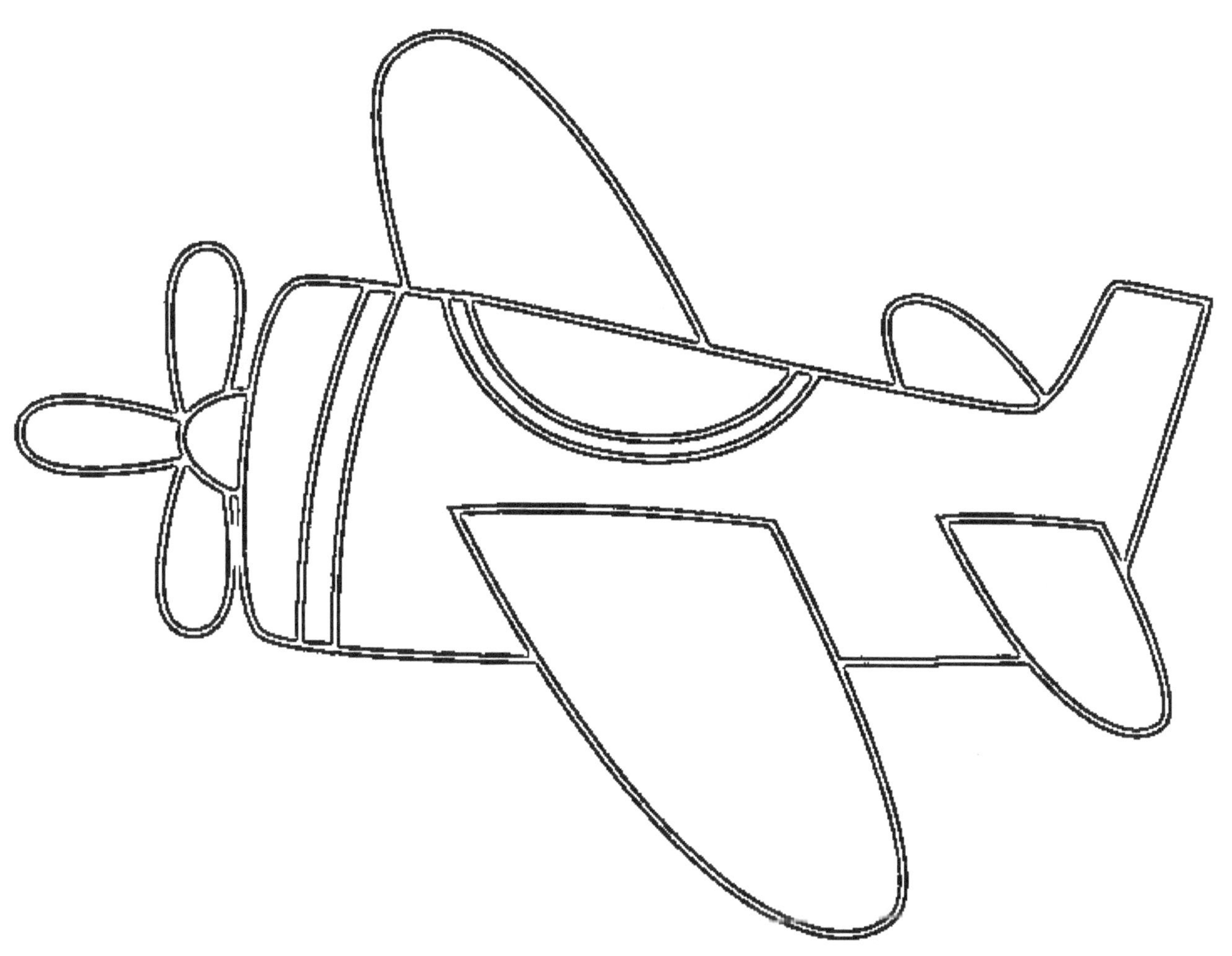

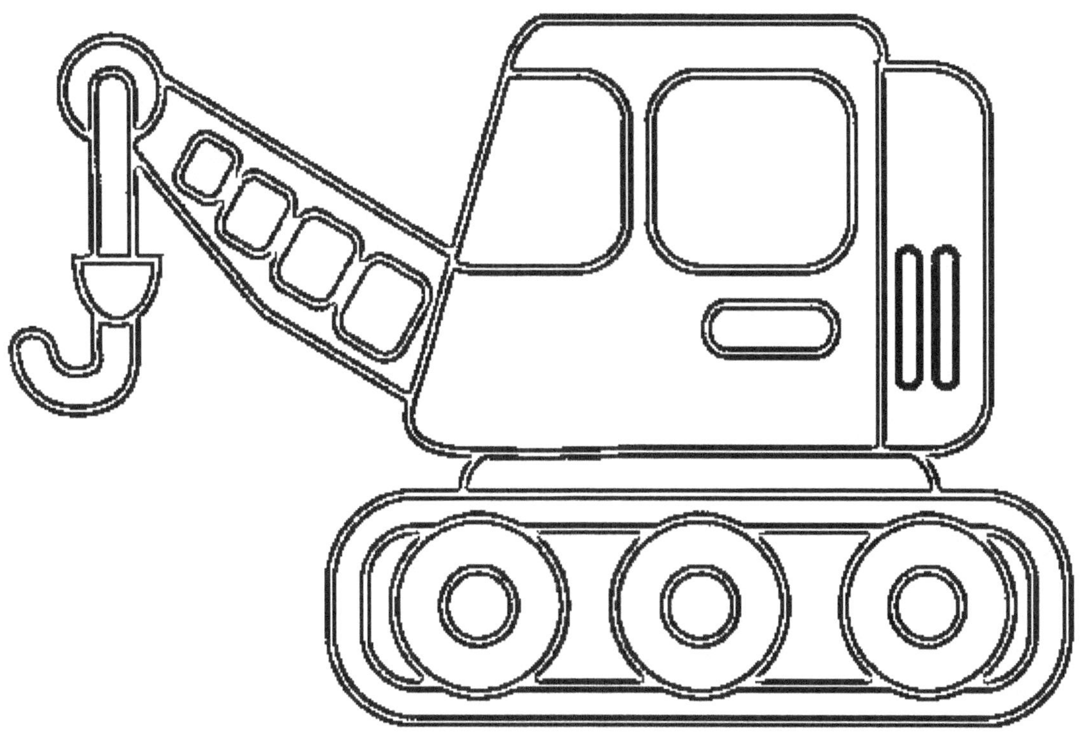

Repaint and colorize it here

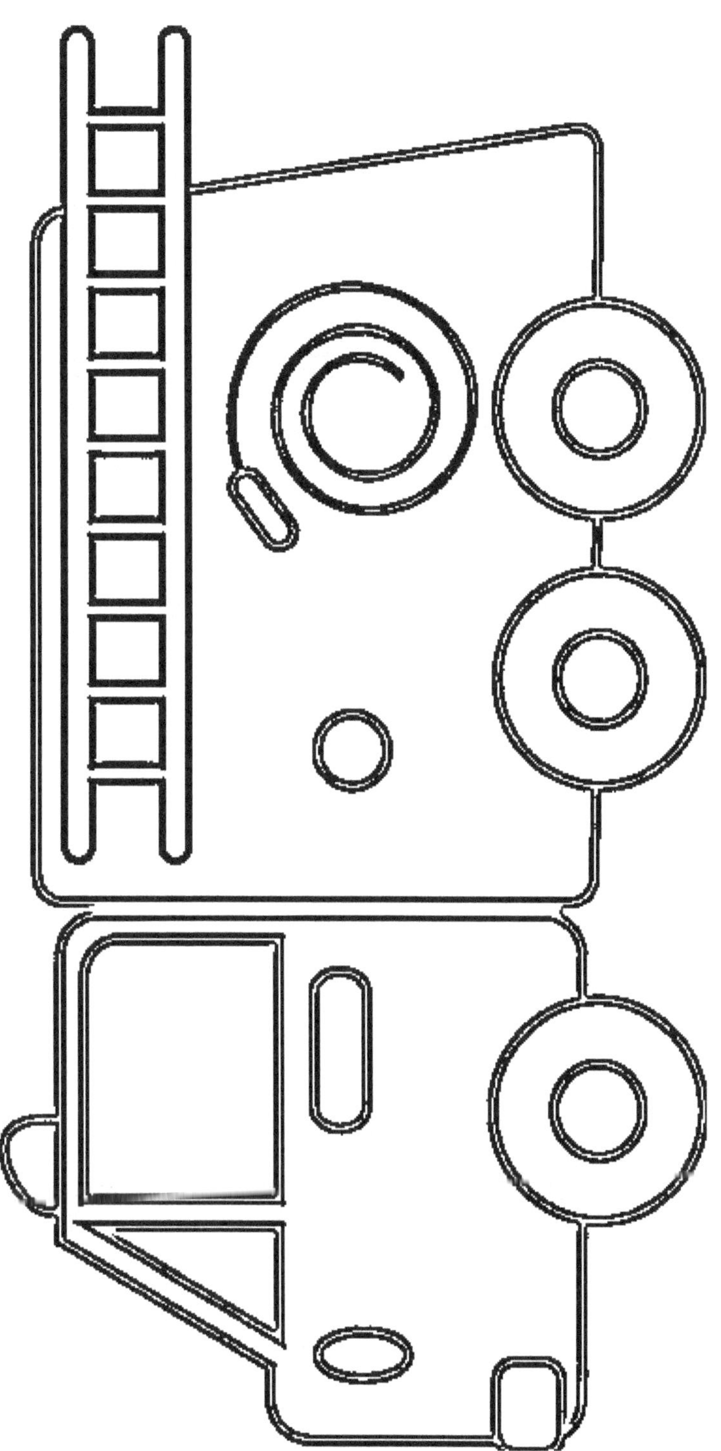

Repaint and colorize it here

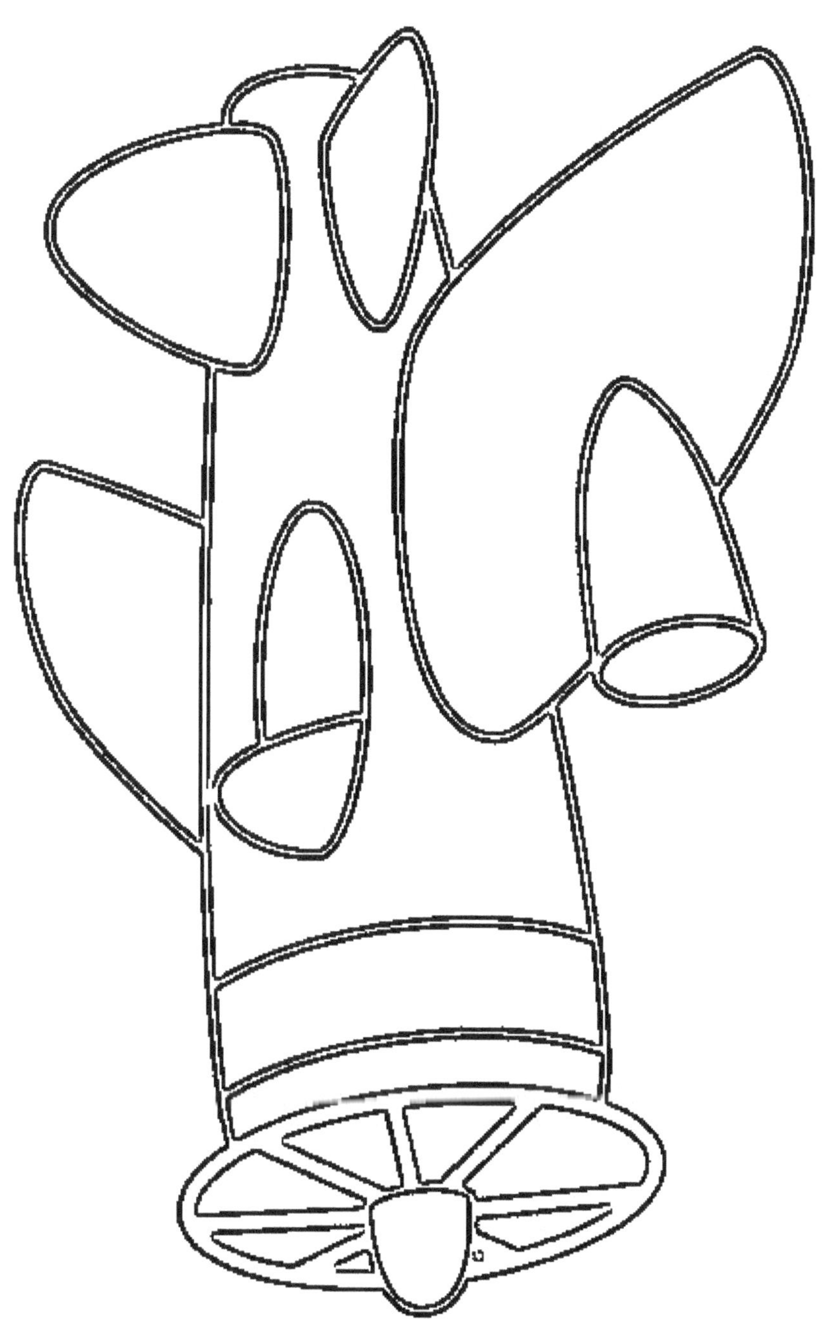

Repaint and colorize it here

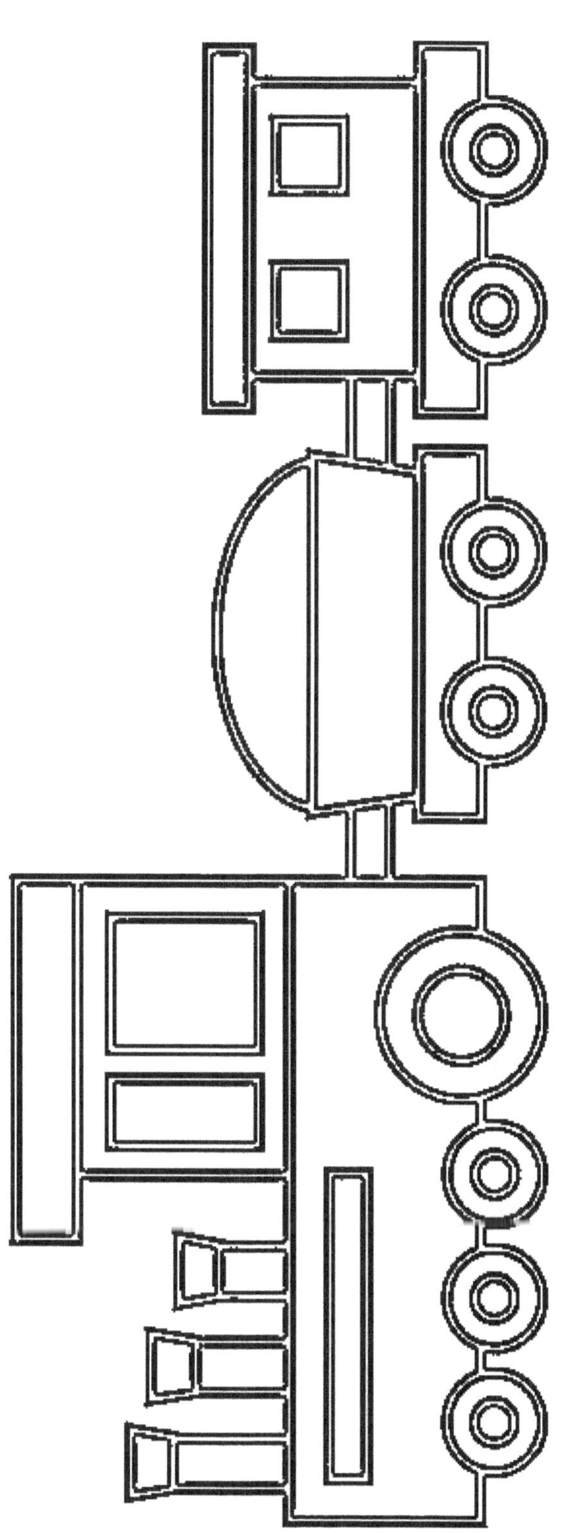

Repaint and colorize it here

Repaint and colorize it here